T0196555

Reconciliation of the Heart

Latasha Smith

authorHOUSE®

AuthorHouse™
1663 Liberty Drive
Bloomington, IN 47403
www.authorhouse.com
Phone: 1 (800) 839-8640

Published by AuthorHouse 07/23/2016

ISBN: 978-1-5246-0204-8 (sc)
ISBN: 978-1-5246-0202-4 (hc)
ISBN: 978-1-5246-0203-1 (e)

Library of Congress Control Number: 2016905567

Print information available on the last page.

Contents

Adulation 1

Adore 2

Never Ending Closeness 3

Joy 4

I wish on a star 5

Candor 6

Here we go again 7

About us 8

Digression from the heart 9

A silent letter to you 10

A beat to my heart 11

Needs 12

No text message 13

I need 2 be 15

Win me Again 17

Small Things 18

Craving The Invisible 19

An Angel brought you to Me 21

Open heart 22

Attention 23

Love is an adventure 24

Short era 26

My muse 27

My darling love 28

Internal love 29

Quiet spark 31

Caress 32

Commitment 33

Hooked on you 34

Sleep don't come easy 36

There goes my life 37

Carried Away 39

Doubt by default 40

Take me Away 42

Beyond Affection 44

Okay 45

SiLeNce 46

I am yours 48

Loving Him 49

Doubt by Intuition 50

Crosshairs 51

Enchantment 52

Far and alone 53

Patience 54

Selling me Dreams 55

Glare 57

Stress for Less 58

Time and time again 59

There's a price to pay 60

Upon a star 62

Stay 64

Distance by thoughts 65

Miss you 66

I can't find 67

Unsteady road 69

Touchless 70

Little did I Know 72

Curiosity 73

Rough 74

The Blood in My Hand 75

Misaddition 77

Red tear drops 79

Away 80

Subconscious 81

What are you Protecting 82

Save myself 83

Yes I hung up on you 84

Beware Of Notification 85

From me to you 86

I'm sorry I was late 88

The one that got away 89

Make it like it was 90

Soul redemption 91

Love is just a word 92

What about me 93

Breathless 94

Roll up the window 95

Never have to be alone 96

Intimacy 97
Ignoring love.. 99
What can never be 100
Difficult.. 101
Ever after 102
The end of the road 103
Wasted my years..104
People change...105
Fearful..106
Ex..107
On defense 108
Hes not coming 110
Let me go 111
Not alone 113
Wondering eyes.. 115
I shall try to love 116
Push away 117
A.L.O.N.E.. 119
Vacation..120
Dismissed... 121
Temporary Forevers 123
All the while.. 124
Shady heart 125
Chew on this 126
Musical Genius..127
Dark Cave..129

Adulation

A brief moment with you creates a wave of satisfaction in my soul.

You say I give you no bad vibes.

And the truth is; I'd never do you wrong because I know how it feels to be betrayed.

The spirit of us together is strong and magnificent.

From the words you speak creates a new outlook for me.

You give hope and some type of irregular heartbeat that I have to breathe deep.

My heart: complicated beyond any other fraction that couldn't be calculated.

There could be more to our story in the future; I want to say we're soul mates:

That this is love, this is as real as adulation can provide us with greatness of persuasion to be an idled couple.

Hopefully no problems will create complications between us.

We provide too much conversation, interest, and sunshine to one another's hearts.

Our relationship is not focused on sex;

But plans:

Plans to make each other successful; we have short days of our friendship that is building, but adulation is knocking extremely hard.

No one can break this, but ourselves, which could never happen no matter the situation.

This creased bond we have is in disposable – my heart is full of adulation

Adore

I see you

I scope you

I know you're sitting in the corner with your shades watching me

I move to talk to my associates and I feel your eyes follow me through my meet and greet.

You stay quiet and irrelevant but quite suspicious.

You were once no one to me

And now you mean the world to me

I tried to dust it off for a long time

I tried to ignore you and your shadiness, but somehow your distance from me drew me to you.

I was so scared of what could be with the steps we took...

And we have so long to go

I'm amazed at the circumstance we've come through and exceeded to

Every day I love you more and more

And I can honestly say you're the only one I can adore

Never Ending Closeness

As wine in a glass is held: As is I would be ecstatic to house myself around you.

There are some kinds of electric bolts that connect my mind to you.

I can always spin my thoughts around you.

When I'm next to you- I hold to your arm because I need a piece of you to hold on to.

I'm not supposed to, but I feel empty without you.

Too many movies, too many cartoons;

I keep thinking that this will end up happily ever after.

But a fairytale is a make believe story where there is never any confrontation.

But of course we've had many disputes

That's what makes us stronger.

You bring me closer to you with your elective honesty.

But we're staying strong.

There's never a time that our love doesn't miss:

I enjoy our never ending closeness.

Joy

Perceive moments that are only smiling
points for the ways of men

Happiness – the reason of give and take

Pressure the multiple explanations

To be in love

To be free of anger and condemn the untrustworthiness

The grin of our heart to rise in the place of our horizon

Not to look sideways and run about in
the likeliness of some decoy

Completed tasks and enjoy our work

Create a place of rest and it can hold on
with spitefulness - then disperse Joy

I wish on a star

This star that I glare at is in the north.

Up, up, away where the tip of my nail points

I know I'd try and reach and cannot touch.

Ability to rise to greater heights is where I've come. I would have thought I'd never make it...

I'd given up and just put in hopes.

My dreams were deferred and dusted under a carpet;

But this one star:

This star that I see in this deep black sky, points out a new leaf for me.

All the things I need to get done with my life can be back on the table

Our drastic change.

My man,

My love:

Has helped me by guiding me and voicing expectations I'd thought I'd never go to

He has achieved so many goals and shown me that initiative is the key to success

Not just dreaming;

So tonight I sit alone.

Looking at the star,

It shines with great illumination and I wish that this man in my life will always be mine forever and ever.

Candor

In all honesty I'm kind of scared

We're compatible and like each other

But being together for one sake

Is it that we can be together forever regardless of ones circumstance?

Can there be more to me and you than arousal

I love your maturity and manliness

I love being with you and held by you

I love the way you sleep because it soothes me

When you hold my hand I feel secured and comforted

Your knowledge is greater than many

And your talent is assertive and impressive

I pay attention to many many things about you

But do you for me?

Could you see me with you till the end?

I'm uncertain and scared how we may turn out because we come from 2 different worlds and you have more experience in life.

You teach me so much, but is it good enough to start our life?

Here we go again

Every night we make sweet love

Rather it last 30 min to an hour

I'll love you forever

We have something special

Something that can never end

It's evolving yet it's such a routine

My thoughts rotate and spin yet I'm not holding nothing in

All I know

We have a way of life

It's so real

So comfortable that I know for a fact

I couldn't go without you as we take this step towards forever

Your love is quick sand

Your convo makes me feel right

Beside you everyday

It makes me smile to say; "Here we go again."

About us

There is no man that can ever be you

There is no man that can ever take me away from you

You are the love of my life

I may not show it like I'm supposed to

But I feel it whole heartedly

Yes

I cried @ the thought and the knowing
of being away from you.

But I know in the end it's for the better

Like you said

To be missed

Every step I take

Every time I blink my eyes

Every toss and turn I make while asleep all that

Pounds my mind is thoughts about us

Digression from the heart

To honor your request and give up who I used to be is the biggest step in life I'll ever have to take

You have mentioned that my priorities are not in order

I've been told that once, but the person was referring to my attitude

The base of who I really am

I thought I had changed up while being away from you for a month, but a mistaken world which I convinced my self

It is no other than the beginning of this transformation of my attitude and unsteady playfulness

In this case in my heart to love you as I do

I am learning to become humble

To walk beside you with grace

I apologize for the old me

But I want us to be one and for you to be the first person I run to

Sometimes I hesitate because I know you're more experienced in life

I just don't want to be judged in the things I may fall to fault at times

But as we both know

It is getting better over time

I wish we could converse more about random events or things that go on, but it almost seems like we talk about everything where there's nothing else to say and it makes me feel empty sometimes because I feel like I have nothing to offer

A silent letter to you

I feel so repelled from you!

But it's only my fault: my disaster I brought from within a wall I created.

I told you I was scared but didn't break the meaning of afraid to you.

Please forgive me for being distant

It's only my heart that hurts from loving you –

It hurts because this fear of losing you is affecting my entire being.

Yes I cry but not from pain but from this dark notion of not being with you.

Maybe in my thoughts

I said too much one thing isn't good.

But that's not true

Yet I feel if I don't have you I feel lonely

Not to know you love me I should just be alone and captivated in the thoughts of everything that is you.

I am beyond fortunate to have you, but to keep how I really how I feel about you and what I want from you to myself.

I will never be right there with you.

A beat to my heart

Music soothes me

It gives me a steadiness to ease my emotions

No matter the genre or the length of the song

I can enjoy someone's art they have put
together to keep them alive and happy

No matter the situation of race of a person

Everyone wants to be happy

Music is in everyone's heart

Whether sad or depressed

It's there

Love helps people grow love gives people a reason to live

Maybe sometimes a purpose

But in general

A life of love is happiness

Needs

Everyone needs a support system

Lost in some episode of emotions, hate, love, or lucrative obsession

Who are we to find someone who can give us their all?

Why is it so hard for people to become as one?

A relationship no matter where it can happen, takes place

We need one another to build a social cycle

Through life we face people who we say that we want or that we crush on.

We desire the need to be fulfilled in a label of marriage.

The relationship status that over powers our loneliness.

We develop the influenced characteristics in what we need in our desire for a person, yet there's a potential of more things that are added.

We don't want but seek to compromise and accept

Settling for what one needs is an abrasion for the heart

It is what we finalize when we have no hope for what could be better.

This is a self-destruct choice for a few, but undeadly.

To step in a world where we are elated to be in love, is what one needs.

There are ways to seal a bond

Yes, it takes a commitment of loyalty, it takes effort, and it takes time, with explosive tactics of transparency to one another's heart.

The intricate for crave, the desire, the togetherness on each other to feed, STARTS-> first with need.

No text message

My phone is silent

My heart is quiet

I wait for your words

But there is nothing

I know you didn't leave me in this vacant moment of time

But I feel so alone cause you left me flapping

Wondering

Lost

In contemplation of where you could be and what you may be up to

Are you waiting for me?

Can you be thinking as hard for me as I am for you?

Each deranged thought for time for each tick on the clock every time I check my phone

I over anticipate your remarks and give you a breath from me

I'm in need of you

I don't mean to smother

But my heart craves you

It is for my interest to step back

But one can't break addiction

There.

I'm telling you all I need is you

Just send me something

Some affection

I am below the emotional roller coaster without your words

I hesitate still to send my words

But I know I drown my necessity of love into your ear...

To your phone

Please text me if you're too occupied to call

I need 2 be

I need to be told I'm worth your time

I need to be held and comforted by you

Please don't draw away when I say I need you to keep me in your arms

Keep me in your arms forever

As these tears stream unaccounted for down my face

I need to smell your skin for support of your love that surrounds me

I need to be told I'm needed by you that I'm your one and only who you never can live without

Say you want me for endless times

Say you can't function on some element without me

I need you to complete me with every word, touch, expression, inside of you.

I beg for you to give me your all but you drain time of the matter.

I need 2 assured that this isn't a game that you're playing.

I need to know this isn't a waste of time that

I'm not a waste of time to you

I need to be told and promised that

You think about me constantly that

My name is always in the back of your mind and imprinted in your soul

I need to be guided in a dance by you to lead me in a romance

Song that plays to the same tune in both our hearts

I need to know if when we are distant you sleep and reach for me when I'm not there

But all else all notions aside I need to be held over and over to rest assure from my heart that you are aware I need to be loved

Win me Again

So you think I will always be yours

You think you one me and that's it

You say you love me and have your brand on my heart

I admit you got my heart some place higher than it's ever been

But we have to keep ascending PLEASE

We know there's so much more to what we have and I am so anxious to get there

But as I look:

As I love you more we are taking love slowly

We're being oh so safe

I admit I have the upmost respect for you

I do

I never want you to think I'm taking you or anything you do for granted

I use to think of only me, but with you we are one and there's never ever ever a moment that goes but that I don't love you or think of you or ponder how wonderful you are

Ask me to be yours forever and trust it will be another grand finale

Whatever, it takes what ever you do

You'll always win me again

Small Things

My composure walking towards you is unsteady

I would have never thought I'd meet someone like you to complete my soul

My soul has become intertwined with your but it is your job to maintain me

Not my love because you'll always have it

Just your responsibility with my heart keep captivating me with the small things

Yes:

I know you don't care for romance, but oh well

You'll grow to understand it

But we must start now before it's too late before we become deeper than what we are

I need your certification of impressing me with small acts of kindness

Some public display of affection

Some special way of a heart racing

Language you may silently show me from across the room

No matter where we are you have to comply with some sexual four play of romance

It will make me as a woman feel wanted

Distance can caused by either one of us but to continue our love is all in the small things

CRAVING THE INVISIBLE

CRAVING THE INVISABLE

OPTIONS ARE APART OF LIFE

BETWEEN TWO

BETWEEN THE ONE DESIRED

AND THE ONE WHO IS A BRUSH OF KINDNESS

DESIRING A GUY WHO'LL GIVE YOU NOTHING BUT EMPTY WORDS AN TESTY SITUATIONS

ONE WHO WILL SAY I LOVE YOU AND VANQUISH IN THE CROWD TO DO HIS OWN THING.

YOU ARE GRATEFUL FOR A GUY WHO WON'T SAY MARRY ME, WHO USES YOU FOR YOUR TIME, AND EMOTIONS.

HE CAN'T COME TO THE TERMS OF APPRECIATING YOU BECAUSE THERE MAY BE SOMEONE ELSE. COULD THERE BE?

HE DOESN'T CALL OFTEN OR SERENADE YOU WITH HIS PRESENCE TO BE CARESSED AND BASKED IN SWEET EXCTASY.

HE IS LOW DOWN, BUT IN AN AQUIRED CUTE WAY?

YOU CLAIM HE'S NOT MISTREATING YOU BUT LOOK AGAIN, HE DOESN'T EVEN KNOW YOUR PHONE NUMBER BY HEART, DOESN'T KNOW YOUR FAVORITE RESTAURANT, DOESN'T CARE TO GO OUT AN SHOW P.D.A.

WHO IS HE TO YOU BUT A FABRICATION OF MISPLACEMENT IN AN INVISABLE RELATIONSHIP WHERE HAPPINESS ISN'T THE GOAL BUT INADEQUATE EMOTIONS.

UNSTABLE TRUTH TO SELF THAT BEING MISTREATED IS APART OF SOMETHING INSIDE YOURSELF.

BAD BOYS? OR JUST CARELESS MAKES YOUR HEART MELT? HOPE YOU DON'T THINK YOU CAN CHANGE THEM.

CAUSE IT WILL BE EX GIRL TO THE NEXT GIRL. ISN'T THAT HOW THEY PLAY? BUT SOME?

HOW DEEP INSIDE YOU WILL ALWAYS LOVE HIM?

UPGRADE TO A PLACE WHERE MR. KIND OFFERS YOU THE WORLD IN A GOLD BOX.

HE CAN GRANT ALL THAT YOU ASK FOR, FROM RESPECT TO LOVE.

DOES HIS ATTENTIVENESS ERK YOU? HE ACCOMMODATES EVERY FEELING YOU HAVE IN YOUR BODY.

MAKE SURE HE IS A MAN THAT IS LIVABLE. QUIT CRAVING THE INVISIBLE.

An Angel brought you to Me

Do you believe is some kind of initial attraction?

Random moments light some type of fire with new thoughts, new beginnings in happy expectations for what didn't happen in the future

You walk up randomly to me while sitting on the beach

You gave me your time and conversation without hesitation

I was flattered

What more could I ask for?

Your attentive spirit towards me after your lengthy introduction

It was warming

I felt like I was in a zone that has never been touched on before

You brought out some rare social antiques that left me astray

I don't talk to people for random moments but as a businessman, I'm aware you're easy for conversation

I fill an Angel brought you to me

Also they use boat so will that I see nothing wrong with being communicatively free

I appreciate you and your openness to be man that blossoms my shyness.

To pick up a friend in a split second is risky

But you...

You're a relief

Open heart

To save the most overlaying words to you

Is often what I try to express

Your looks give me an exert of alteration from every blink I take in from you

How tiresome I feel is a relief in lying beside you...

I keep blinking to awaken myself to reestablish my lustful thoughts of you

Yet is seems to be greed of undeniable doubt

Well

A taste of doubt

But for my own emotions

I cast away

You alert my heart with your sensation of elegance

I try so hard to rise upon your difficult yet irrational spell you've whipped me into

I can only open my heart to you because you make me feel out of the ordinary

You are my insight like my second voice in my head

There is no one but you and you ravish my soul with completion of space

Just to be in 2 different places alters my emotions

Cast my tear into the ground

But have been knows you are my love

I really hate for us to be apart

This is why to you my love I open my heart

Attention

One verb that everyone caters to, sometimes attention is never given enough

To be so selfish in wanted every view of your eyeball focused on me is the way I think it should be, but I know can't happen

To be in your spotlight spot light is quite fantastic to me

You fascinate me not only in your words but in your doings

You motivate me to strive and achieve just as you've done

Sometimes when we're together I still feel lonely

Like the focus isn't on me

Like you don't even care that I'm there

Just please reassure me that you love me and express your feelings to me so I will know that we are everlasting

Yes actions do speak louder than words

But your words in my ears circulate my blood and make my heart race

If you leave me in suspension: just know to grasp me use your love

Captivate my attention

Love is an adventure

An uneventful place to be after all falls down the fun

The impression

What

Yes love is the place to be

Everyone needs someone to make them feel

Feel

Feel love; or wanted or like the world revolves around them

To roll from one emotion

To hop scotch how one feels because of the treatment that's being given

The lost feeling comes and you feel like gagging getting every rid of the thought of love in your gut

Some motion picture this is

Yes infatuation is there but this alone feeling is not even there its just empty

Empty like in my calls and voicemail

The questions where you at and what you doing are endless

But I'll let it pass cause you making me lose my mind and I hate you for it

Moving on is not an option

It's not much is at stake but it's enough for me to be confused

This is the wrong deal

This talk to the hand portrait you putting out is worthless to yourself because you're losing out

It's funny of your worst fear. Ha

I hope you get sick; because that's what you get, I'm suffering and your living

It's whatever

I'm a be free

I'm a shine and be the hot commodity that's untouchable

I thank you for helping me be put in the limelight the place of exertion to be on top and had me somewhere else love yes it is yes you brought me out in the role coaster is almost over it visionary of this haunted house of forever with you chuckle my way to go in circles with how much we are supposed to be I'm looking bad saying we will be together for eternity stuck on a Ferris wheel

Yo, whatever; I'm a be me such a changed you got it begun my heart for being in love is like having a career why is love and adventure

Short era

To prove you care for someone is to hold to them all night

You hold them to their sorrows in her Houghton improves your strength of time you spend with them of some

It may be fabricated but it's what they need

What they have

Never had answered on the verge of the meaning of love

Holding someone can create the window for love, yet the person that's doing the holding may brush emotions away into never

To them they could be doing something positive in a very short era

Once a player always a player: no settling for them

Just him learning what to get for women by identifying their most needy and vulnerable moment

He can lie he can play pained, but whatever it may take to get from her

Only in the short era

My muse

He makes my heart stand out of my chest

He gives me the forced thought to be bold

He has an arrogance that captures my feelings

But it's doomed from the beginning

A different side of me he brings out

Like a place of enthusiasm that I missed so clearly

The desire that he gives me is very remarkable

But ways of thoughts are on unreliable

Hurt always come in all relationships

Whether it be friendship or love ships

There's always a type of blockage

An error somewhere in the aura of what could have been,

An error of destiny complicates everything

The way I'm caught up my heart would have to choose

Could I be?

Am I falling for my muse?

My darling love

Is it in me to express your masculinity?

It's in my heart that I want you

You brighten the universe just by existing

You are my hope for being the stance of all I believe

You are the most delicious man that I want

You are the only person there makes me feel enlightened of such

Decorate my world my darling love

Sweet one with soothing grace

I pray favor from my life into your heart

I see us together in eternity

My darling love you I love you so much

Being with you forever is the greatest gift

I know it's a long time but in history it's obvious we fit

There is nothing in this world that you can sub

Baby, cause I'll never let you go

You're everything to me my darling love

Internal love

Hi! I seeing you from afar as I step into class

I didn't want to speak, I didn't want to look

But in the midst of my shadow I saw your face

I saw you

My loving hero or

I can't be without you

I feel so empty and destitute without you

You light up my world and make me smile

You're the most precious gemstone in my life

I wish I can express more

But I will pour my heart out to you by the litters, a love overflow

When you're not there, I think of you

I love you; I dream and fantasize about you

All your encouraging words and your thoughtfulness is in my mind

Like a panther in the night, you stole my heart, you stole my kindness

You added them to your smile and your heart

To give my all to you is the best ever

It what I've always wanted

You're my northern star and my teddy bear

The feelings I have for you are greater than what I've ever known

When you pull me close I feel secure

I feel your warm sweet lips on my shoulder my neck and my mouth

As you hold me close never ever let me go

Make me your lover make me your wife

You are the only one I want to spend with the rest of my life

You're cute, you're lovable, and you're unique

I will never be ashamed of you.

I will and can hold my head up high with love, respect, and pride in you

Quiet spark

I don't know if I can live without you

I have my thorough thoughts about you

But you make me feel so free and relaxed

I'm appreciative you for all you do

I'd never thought I'd be in love with something of your stature

You have a mellow fun lovable personality

You keep me in check and motivate me in many ways

You are so intelligent with multiple ways of solving life

But I still don't know if I can trust you

I don't know how to take it

I mean my trust level is so low but only because I see your friends and what they do

The question is, will you do that to me?

I can't fight this and you treat me so right, but that's where my second guessing plays

I'm so scared and you just live and do what's necessary like it's a movie all the basic things, but where's my flowers and candy and small surprises?

Where's my "I love you" notes or romantic gestures

We're so original with no pizazz

I hurt because of these things others do

It doesn't have anything to do with us, but I don't want to be like that

Like a bland love with no spark

Caress

Now you know what's up... when you pick me up;

I'm feeling you from head to toe:

I love the way you feel and that fo'sho.

I ain't got time to play no games.

It's me and you all the way.

Your body is so right against mines.

We whisper quietly cause it's so much to say.

You holding me in:

Captivating my heart racing moments and the way your tongue feel in my mouth give me sensation.

Your hands are so Strong, yet so soft.

The way your heartbeat on my chest is graceful to the point where there's no stopping:

There's no rest.

Your kisses are luscious,

Yet, like and our closeness of intimacy is a point where we give our might – to keep it up until daylight

Cause that's how it supposed to go.

Commitment

I've been paying attention to you over awhile now.

I feel like there's something that attaches me to your soul

I could see myself with you forever.

I could love you like you need to be loved and I would dedicate my heart to you, if you would do the same.

Your words, your character, and your loyalty to society makes me think you're heaven sent

You and I for certain can build to love with the greatest commitment

I see within your eyes past pain as horrid as mine, but looking deeper, you desire me just as much I crave you.

Your actions show me that you are just as willing to step in bliss where your heart is with me and I should be your supplement

You say we need more of each other and I agree – it can be commitment

Hooked on you

When I lay my head down

I can only dream of you

Fantasies, thoughts, wants of you control my imagination

To belong to you and no one else

Cultivates my heart with hope that it could last forever

To be covered in love with your words: with your meaningfulness

You are my emotional heater

How can you pull me in your swirl of gracefulness and all these to make us feel so true?

This sudden pull and attraction of your voice makes my heart tremble with excitement

Yet there is a darkness that frightens me of the unknown you

There's something there that I still don't know and it scares me

I promise I have nothing to hide: but you? You, I know you do.

It's ok cause one day as we grow and grow to love each other

There will be a time for our hearts to blend

But as far as we are now

I am hooked on you

You make me feel some kind of way

The incredible belief in what we have

And what we are to one another

Makes me parallel my emotions to you

I am known to be quiet

I am known for my sufficive attitude but no matter what I say

No matter my mood

I am officially hooked on you

Sleep don't come easy

No plans

I feel so empty

Thoughts of you are a deep distraction

To lay there without you beside me is a disgust in life

I'm uncomfortable and disgruntle with an uneasy feeling that tightens around my temple for the same kind of pressure to keep hoping that you were there

Tossing and turning and sliding

I reach unknowingly for your fingers but I cannot fulfill the space

We are one but only in the back of my mind

You my other half is waking me without being here

The fragrance of you after a hot shower

The warmth of your brown delicate skin

I cannot close my eyes and drift in peace

While I cannot feel and know these things are absent

But after time goes and I close my eyes again I only see me

I do what I can to sleep & listen to music

But right now sleep don't come easy

There goes my life

On the way to something new

I ascend

Yes I am lifted

I fall

You took my hand and escorted to me to your words of perfection

These words flow like butter in a desert.

But you know where I'm going

This is how I fade to the background

But then I come out

You keep me on my toes

Yea I fall

And I realize it's me

I break to anger easily

I'm sorry

Misery

It's an acquire asset I learned from someone

Its regret

I have it

But I'm pushing it away

Far away

Slowly I'm coming to myself

My reality

Your world

Now I have to share our worlds

Come closer

Please let me whisper to you that

I'm caught up

Please let me whisper to you that I'm caught up

I got to stop this split forecast I have

I thank you for putting me on to what is what

No matter the situation you keep telling me professionalism

A lay keeps her man in good taste

At this game I'm new

I used to do what I want and that was it

But I let you go

I give it away to you

It may sound unnatural but without you I would still be wasting my time not doing anything promising for my womanhood for my maturity level to increase

I wasted time and energy living life not trying to impress anyone and stayed in the spotlight

Didn't care what the world said

Instead

You changed that

I keep climbing to higher heights and one day I'll meet my standards and yours

I'm giving up my past to better my future

I'm doing this for the best of me

Of Us

What's right?

There goes my life

Carried Away

A woman needs?

A woman desires?

What can a man see to pull his potential mate?

In a man's eyes he watches and preys to see her credentials

What can this woman do for him and can she last & emotionally satisfy him

Credentials: to say a man has a list of things he expects

When he finds her

Will he approve?

Ha ha, he continuously gives her appreciation for her choosing him

Appreciation of what a woman does is vital

No one likes to be a unnoticed after continuously giving their all

Let a man get carried away with proof of his love and she will be grateful

A woman craves attention she is drawn to her man's needs for his attention

As she holds her integrity she holds her man

Together they can calculate the equivalent description of each other's happiness

Being infatuated with one another and keeping it forever can never be under balance to get carried away

Each other's love is charismatic and full of quality

It comes so natural

Real love is not a charade

Maybe it's something that can actually take place where they come together and it happens to be fate

Yet, for all eternity in love let them both be carried away

Doubt by default

Marriage won't change it?

All the love we have

All the time we spend; evolving to a higher level of closeness

Wouldn't marriage be the next step?

I'm not putting anything against it

Are you ready to give up your fast life? To put up with
all the extras you might have on the side.

Are you down for loyalty honor and respect for the rest of your life?

Yes, for the rest of your life

Did that send chills through your spin?

My associates said once we: once you and I have it all before marriage,

That you would love me just the same or less, not more

It hurt to hear him say that about us

I take that as his opinion, but I let it get to my thoughts
and now my thoughts are out of whack

I feel that you would love me more through time

I feel in my heart, it will grow but it's completely on you

I know we started out rocky because I ignored you, but I gave in to the
thought that maybe it's worth taking a chance and not being afraid of love

To get rid of my quote that love was a figure of my
imagination and that no one would love me

But being with you proves that love exist

That there is love for everyone

Even though we don't speak on marriage

I do think on it but in the end it will be your grand choice to choose
me I just hope that we will not be like anyone else in unhappiness

Every day is a day that you are first on my mind and give me
your protection with proof of standing up for me

I appreciate you and I have not shown it much in public and from my heart

I'm sorry

We are supposed to be best friends yet I don't even think
that we have really reached that point Sometimes I wish we
can expand our vocabulary in our conversations

I do feel bad when we sit for long periods without talking

I guess because it seems we talked about almost everything but we haven't

You were right, we do have a long way to go

And since we are continuing this journey

Easy to tough we must hold hands through it all

1 step, 2 step, twenty steps at a time

I don't know why it would seem so hard; but I assume of
circumstances of the world we came together in

At this moment I just want to dig my head in your chest and intertwined my
fingers with yours and cry cuz I'm happy but scared of what's to come for us

The way in my soul: I don't want to live without you,

But I'm ready to listen to you tell your heart…
although time… in due time we will see

I'm in love with you and want to give you my all it is only
the truth to admit I have doubt by default

Take me Away

Some guy came to me in the club

Yes he was talking in my ear

I was already feeling good

I was really feeling pleasant

Nah, he ain't caught my eye

But my homegirls were laughing

So yes, you heard right

The man was trying to talk to me

Give me the 411 on his lifestyle and what all else he was working with.

Me? Haha yeah, you know me

I sure was listening

I was bored and tipsy

So I gave him the time of day

Don't get mad he not worth me leaving you for

That's out of the question

Hmm that's why;

Why we shouldn't even be at the same club, but whatever

I'm gonna have fun

I'm feeling good, but yeah, the guy was
talking about all his money he got

Everything in his name he got paid off

I guess he paused to see if I had something to say

I didn't

So he kept going

He liked foreign lands and talking about taking me away

Away from this boring town and same routine of life everyday

Ha! Something I heard for the first time, but he still kept going; asking me where I wanted to go and what I should and could see

This dude was trying to bait me hard

I said I'm in a good place thanks

He was like well I thought all girls want to be taken away

I laughed and was like,

"I'm a lady baby so it's something's you can't do to pull real women away, especially with my man standing across the way. I'm sorry if you thought this was a date but my man about to take me away good day."

Beyond Affection

Hey baby,

Today is a very special day for you and I'm glad I am by your side to accompany you through it.

It is destiny that we are together.

You forever will rock my world.

I've been liking you since the first time d saw you.

You make me so happy.

When I see you: I can't take my eyes off you.

When I'm with you: I don't want to let you go.

And when I hear your voice: I can't be still.

You're so sexy and you make me feel warm inside.

I know we been together for a Short time.

Strait up.

You are the best I'll ever want and ever have.

When you leave I miss you so.

And baby just to let you know, as time continues there much affection we can show.

Okay

I have no problem with you

It's just the things you do be killing me

I'm doing what I know is best

But hey babe what you think?

Sometimes I feel like it's a test

You want so freaking much from me

I'm doing my best not to be superficial or fake

Yet deep down inside I'm like okay

I'm surprised you haven't realized I'm down for whatever with you no matter the danger

And with you I don't have to worry about the danger

You won't even let me get close to fire

But deep down inside I'm still your lady ride and die no matter the circumstance

I love you so much

I'm not worried about my fate

Every time you walk in the room and smile and talk about good times in my heart I say it's okay

When you're out on your grind most of the night I get angry I get hateful and feel like I despise you

But you have to understand I don't like to be alone without you

As you climb higher in your popularity is great for your sake

I feel like I'm being selfish and I know it's what you want and what you've been needing

So my tears expressed ok

SiLeNce

Current mood: cold

Category: Romance and Relationships

Hush

Let me speak

Let me talk

Well then no go ahead say what you got to say?

Hope it ain't nothin smart allic

Somethin insensitive

What you scared of the dark

You tryin to hide somethin in ya heart

Look I gave up something precious for you

So I know you got more to say then how you rollin ya eyes

Why you got to be like this

Why can't you speak for real?

I see your mouth

Somethin that's precious to me

But I'm still talkin cause you can't say nothin

What you holdin back

You want to write it out

Look time is of essence

And I'd give all mines for you

What you got to say about that?

Nothin ...? For real?

So if I go played the game

You couldn't get mad

Cause you ain't talkin you ain't given me the time of day

But that's just it

How many times I got to say I don't want nobody else

Damn what I got to do

Shit delete all my contacts an just keep you in there

Hell I'd do it

But u wouldn't tell me to

I'm still runnin my mouth tryin to concentrate on every detail of you

But you not hearin me

You not wantin me

You don't have nothin to say huh

Still: well

I guess that's my answer

Silence

Is that what you got for me?

Huh

Yea ok

Still nothin

After all

You are in my heart

You are my love

But still silence

sshhhhh

I am yours

For whatever it may seem

You mold my hear with your words

You've done what no other man has stepped to do

You've given me your time and love

You've been patient and vital with me

I am to you

YOU

Always grateful even though I act ruggish at times

I'm learning to be who I am

Even though I know I can't have everything @ the time I ask for it:

You do in your power what you can to fulfill my request and my needs

And from crevice of my heart I love you indefinitely.

From all of myself to you I give.

Without you I feel tormented and vacant from my body – my world is deeply disorientated without you and I may be crowding you

But please understand me – understand my words

I am yours

I would never give my soul and heart to no one else just because.

I belong to you and every day as we continue – even in frustration out of pain and sweat from my pores we love more and more

Compatible: circumstances: and compromise without you.

I am forever and will be forever torn we are made for each other no matter the uncommonness of scores-

For you my love my life

I am yours

Loving Him

To be in love is something wonderful.

To be infatuated and it's given back to you is a fairytale.

To give your all and your heart to the one you are in love with is amazing.

To think too much beyond trust can be very stressful.

Yet, open your mind to a new world of happiness.

Let rumors and jealousy fade from your heart.

I know I have a jealous spirit no matter the situation, and I try not to let it show…

But it does somehow show in my body language.

I am one of a kind and I love a man one of a kind.

I gave him my heart and I give him my all.

I will never betray his trust nor block him from the truth.

He is my King and the motivation for me to be the woman that I need to be as I am Queen.

I do apologize for my apathetic, rude, and isolated attitude and spirit, it is only because I had lost my way and thought too much into the agony of me being disoriented by to many people telling me different things at once and close people I know living a life style that I disliked.

I can no longer tolerate people who are ignorant and blindsided by something they think they can have but it's so obvious that they cannot or not working for.

I learned if you don't have some type of plan for your life … at least a foundation… then what is there to live for?

Love has to be mutual and it takes the right attitude to keep it afloat and it takes time to continue knowing each other.

Yet, to know that the future holds what you both planned separately and can bring it together is great.

Two souls meant to be will become one no matter the silence between the two.

It's comfortable and slightly odd, but just to know that both hearts are in sync; that makes love a great world to be in with one another.

Doubt by Intuition

I knew that I would be first in the world of unity

Unhappiness creates a doubt for success and my heart was caught in it

To alter the changes of one's usual antics into a fabricated world of Love Hurts

Not getting what I asked for or needed created the doubt and by far built resentment

I needed something every woman deeply craves,

Maybe it is just me and what I define of actions that complete true love.

Knowing what I want was grave and repeated many times

Until one day one man changed it for me

One man held me with no denying my soft skin against his

Who would have thought my intuition of someone else providing me with the key to my exile of unhappiness?

He may have not gotten out of it

Out of my words

Out of my emotions

But he gave me enticed emotional restoration

A deep woman's secret is her emotions and the longing to be touched in a way that makes her body quiver with a man who offers it with no hesitation

He is great for lonely moments, good love, and great conversation

I surely gave doubt my intuition

Crosshairs

To make love to someone in your dreams can put you in an awkward place

To underestimate your feelings for a person that you just met recently can be a slap in the face

To see him amongst his friends and keep an eye on you at the same time is impressive

Spending the short-led time with him is something you can take for a blessing

How dare the heart break if you were to fall in love with him and he not with you?

What world of self-hate could you withstand to not want to ever wake up again from his warm body against yours again?

Slithering in between the crosshairs to find what is exactly right for my soul to be at comfort

Hearing him breathe as we sleep as he cuddles my body makes me crave him more

The liable speeches he gives me can be as great as rain falling through the universe

His words pour unattained truth to my soul to want him as my own is quite illogical and impossibly unfair

My only thoughts I can't admit to him are stuck in crosshairs

Enchantment

Crimes of passion the heart being stolen

Stolen

Kidnapped: scooped up by infatuation

Love taken into a new world

Happiness

Splendor of security

To know someone is corresponding to emotions as such

Taken into a race of intense wonderment where second guessing and thought of everlasting loyalty is evaluated simultaneously

What is there to expect from this roulette of charisma.

To see the smile in his eyes as if he's satisfied but he doesn't seem full of fascination as my heart is

he said he wouldn't be with me if he wasn't happy, but I would think he would have enticed me if he said he wouldn't be with me if he wasn't in love with me

To know that this could last forever

It will only take time

More attracting occasions

Spending excessive time together

He spoils me with his assurance of steadiness

To keep me lighthearted in bliss

He enchants me with his voice, his lectures, and good insight

I pray that it continues to fill my heart with trusting delight

Far and alone

A whole different world is where we are

24 hours a day giving our time to this job and no time for each other

Space

Miles

In some away city is not helping

My thoughts of you

I need you

Oh

Oh so bad

But missing you is hurtful, long, and some kind of emotional condition to our hearts

I don't know how, but in the way I may feel is so jealous and so aggravated that I miss you more than many things I may have done for fun

You my love is what I can't wait to reunite with

To give you and you give me a controlled free amount of our combined time together

To give into aggravation would most likely kill us

But love rides all this notion of emptiness without yo

It is wrong for me to be mad that we are apart I listen to you talk on the phone while we look to each other so distant in a park

But as I know we are far and I am alone

Patience

Sometimes I think it's a dream

You're the one I always will need when we're
a distance from one another

I know I have selfish thoughts

Cause I want you to be next to me at all times forever

But you know I always feel caressed in your love

You sent me in a path of the lady likeness

Sometimes I have trouble but I'm still learning

I do my best to keep up in what you like and
what I can maintain for myself

Sometimes I get angry

Sometimes I get you irritant

But your eyes and kiss melts my animosity away

But you ease my soul to put me in a place of tranquility

I see that I'm not in the place I want to be but I'll get there

Just a few adjustments just be patient with me

Like I'm being patient with you

Selling me Dreams

See the stars in the sky?

You see how the clouds slowly rotate across the moon.

My heart has no place to be but with you

You tell me that you love me

You work for the best of the both of us

But some way it doesn't see fit to this unexcited yet wrecked illusion

When I'm away from you and out among Galant crowds

Because of the rubber necks around me who stare and strike conversation hit my mind and irritatingly annoy me.

Do you see the same thing they seeing me or do they see the same thing you see in me

I feel that others are poisonous to my surroundings so I stay to myself an immediate to jump to the defense and hit the feistiness rather quickly

I swing with you here on this hammock and absorb your jealousy of what I'm saying and replenish my heart that you swear you care and will do your best to be my all.

I noticed your hand is gripped as we sway and I fantasize of the key to my heart is imprinting itself in your hand

As we make all these plans and I hear you talk about what will take place

For the record you're selling my soul a good dream

You're admitting you are the miracle I need in my life

Keep talking with your honest thoughts that you'll be right here when I call your name

Could you here the want in my quivering voice?

When I blink my eyes and look at yours can you feel the uneasiness from me?

You make me so many promises

I'm scared when you don't do them

From my heart I don't know if I could accept you

Redeem them

But as of right now you're selling me dreams

Glare

Splendid is how I explain you

Your words are a cyclone that whisk me off the ground into your strong arms

I'm caught in your eyes

They give off a radiance of caring and new promises of a spectacular future for us both

Your glare takes charge of every drop of sweat from my body

Unstable is what I am when I see you watching me walk with the knowing of your devotion to please my body

Through your glare my realization became fear

The curiosity of some awkwardness of the tightness when you hold my hand

Then to become distant lovers is a blast of common sense due to the environment

Yet, I can be in one place away from you

Away from your stare but my heart is in your hands.

Do I Captivate you am I fly in your mind?

I can only think that our love is contagious to each other.

To give our affection and attention to one another is based on our communication of needs

We base our emotions off of principle but what for?

Let shine

Let's collide

Let's cut back the hold back

Let's caress

Love and share...

Keep on taking me in

With you securing our love in your beautiful manly eyelashes and glare

Stress for Less

I'm feeling so tense

So unhappy

Work is a mindless place of inconsiderate dorks and I need to clock out

I need to be home I can't wait even though I know your work comes first

I can't wait to be sitting right on you

I can defuse and you listen with so much love

I mean I know you don't care

But I appreciate you hearing me out letting me be free in your arms

Oh to relax in your presence is some sort of freedom

A long day is not the word but all I could think of is home

Is you

These people don't run me

You do

You digress my stress you make me exert all
crunch of muscles to a sweet feeling

All I need to do is to get away and get some rest

Your voice soothes my throbbing head

Home with you is stress for less

Time and time again

Time and time again I screw up

It may be at random moments

But it seems to happen

I don't mean to

But if it's my personality then I am relinquishing it

Your jealousy does not surprise me because I'm extremely jealous of things you may not look at me and adhere too.

But I am hurt by your antics

I am too fragile for some of the things you do

Even though you state the things you dislike that I do

I go out of my way to change them because that's what love does

Yet, you tell me to accept who you are and when I mention and want you to change things that I don't like; you don't

You write it off like I never said it

Yet:

Time and time again we have our disputes and I'm learning that you're only making this sort of a one way street

I may change my ways for the better of us and appearance, but just because you claim you're a gentleman doesn't mean you're doing it right

So time and time again we'll talk until we get it right

There's a price to pay

I am taking up in the love that you share with me

Your attitude and demeanor is so strong and your words are always in an honest advice

But I am an idiot not to listen to you and to know you're always right still hasn't cleared in my skull

I may not be here all the way in maturity to understand our compliance knowledge combined

I am working in my heart so hard to get there but I have no idea why I'm not getting it

And when I mess up you always have something to say

For me there is a price to pay

I'm so addicted to you

It's so bad my friends ask is it mutual

I feel it is

But the way you act in public is not as strong

Maybe I need to increase my PDA so you can understand how much more TLC I need

I know you give your all but I feel there is much more

I guess is always perfect in the start but it's becoming Rocky and it's my fault for the things I do and say

Like I lost control

I don't know why I thought this way was a piece of cake

But with my attitude there's a price to pay

For us to keep moving up

Compromise is intact but for the most part I will always follow your moves

When I stray away; PULL me back

After it's all said and done no matter what let us both be in each other's heart

I don't take advantage of us

I'm not a gold digger but I need to be cared for

Money to make my appearance look good for you

Presentable everyday

Yes

Baby with all things in life there's a price to pay

Upon a star

I don't want to call you and seem desperate

Desperate to show you I still love you

Want you

And adore you

I think of you every moment of the day

At night I wish to dream of you

Looking out on the stars

I draw your face

But the brightest of them in the Scorpio distant from the Taurus

It is the star I gaze upon like the twinkle in your eyes

The star twinkles just as bright

To stare at it

Is like staring in your eyes all night

Remembering the warm hugs and caresses

Your head against my chest and mine against yours

Was sweet for me to hear your heartbeat

The hope for always and forever

You cut out my heart and threw it away on the other side of the sky

So my lonely evenings

I sit and gaze at the sky

For the one darkening connection I feel close to you

Upon that star is where my eyes lock

Tears fall from memories of the profile and love

But to look away only increases my pain

As I wait for myself to drain the anguish from my soul

I hold your picture by my pillow by

My heart

The last night I look upon a star and let the past disappear with cries of hurt

I let the reminisce vanish

I love you so much to move on and let you go

So upon this star I wish

Stay

Alone tonight?

Again

I need some tender very precious feeling of your breath against my skin...

I crave love

The words to slip from your tongue and melt my brown skin into your hands

Care please of my wants

Of every way to hold me through the night

Not for a while but every hour until the morning

Until the sunrise please stay

No pressure but let it be constitutional

Let us both come together in expressed desire for one another

You feel as I feel

Are my hands that lay on your hand making your mind change?

I think so

You know you want to stay

For what we have become

As late as it is now I like the way you are making me feel

You help me release my pain

Throughout the night and into the day

I thank you for comforting me and staying

Distance by thoughts

Waking myself out of a dream is the worst thing I can do with the thoughts of you in my mind a rapid.

Rapid

Wet

And wanted

You're so far away and I miss you with all my body

You make my soul cry for your presence

Even though we are not one

I can only dream that we could be

You somewhat have me hypnotize

I've moved on

My loyalties want to only lie with you

The moment I see you all else is irrelevant

My tunnel vision is on just to you and your words

Your eyes

And your body

I want to reach for you and draw you near my face and hold you in my heart

My insides conquer you in my dreams

And yet I still have to realize that you aren't my own

Your distance by thoughts hurt me

But it's only good for us

I want you for my own

I want you because you make me feel free

You are what I need and you have my heart caught

But its only distance by thoughts

Miss you

First I would like to apologize to you for my quiet obvious attitude

I love you endlessly

But the promise from me is real and without you I am broken

I try to stand whole

It is so hard

I can hear your voice and see your picture

Even though you and I both know

It's not the same

It is impossible

It can only be some kind of anger that builds in my soul to be away from you this long

I know you seem annoyed by me but trust me babe your thoughts are probably 10 times in my mind

Some type of endless questionnaire concerning you

I just think of missing you with my entire body

Would constitute this pain of distance

I really miss you

I got it bad

And I'm embarrassed to say that my soul is obsessed with you so much that I feel like we're falling apart

I know it's bad to say it

My whole life is off track

I don't want us to fall off I want us to remain together without any mishaps

I can't find

I'm undeniably lost

My world has been turned into shattered pieces

I may be quick to pick myself up

But my thoughts are inconclusive

My life was shaken up at one point

Set up to fail not by my own choice

I had to start over with minimal support

My world is a mudslide and now I can't find my stabilization

Where am I supposed to stand?

I'm alone because of all the candle lights that the
significant other blew out of with his lies.

I am on the verge to tip forward and be great

Who can stop me even if I'm bound to a bum?

I can't find my sanity to elaborate happiness

I couldn't even tell you what I want or need to make me smile

I avoid depression with work

I avoid emotions with dip in alcohol

I can't find my heart to give to cares of the recklessness of others

I have become withdrawn

I have become a shadow

Never the feeling to satisfy myself necessities

I live to stay awake for others

Just because it's my job

How should I turn my world around after this
heinous crime done with in my marriage?

I had deleted all the emotions from this person
and referred back to my antisocial past

Unlikely for a perky person like me

But I can't seem to even find my way to
words that describe my anguish

All I can do is wish the person who caused me to feel like crap

I wish he'd die

No regrets of that thought.

That's just how I see

My deep emotions crawled in a cave coming
out to prove hate is built and exist

There's no stopping my warpath

By reevaluating and cutting off the cause of pain

I can

But for the future of relationships and the best
of my emotions for someone else

I just can't

Unsteady road

The instance of tonight marks my words for some type of joke

I have done wrong and do not regret it for the sake of myself loneliness

A man of the same ordeal has shown me that is
possible to be treated like a fellow companion

With his words and actions he does not boast in Pride, pity and
annoyance but his mind swims with wonder happiness and honesty
such a man of this nature deserve my time such a man of interest
pay every bit of attention to me and lets me talk freely as he knows
my mind is an ocean and each molecule needs to be relinquished

My words may not make sense to him but he irons
out my spoken thoughts from theories

I have into answers who has done that for me

No one being in the words of a man and being called stupid for having
my thoughts branded for stupidity is the chain my new friend has
broken not I to be made fun of put down and hushed to a scold

Someone who loves you proves that he can
straighten and rebuild your unsteady Road

Touchless

When I need something I have to have it

The concern

An empty intimacy zone is dangerous to repeat over and over again

Did I need or feel a certain type of way is very sad

I may seem hard or like a gangster but honestly I'm simple down to earth and required just one thing to be touched

The soft delicate way of the man's hands the caress of his body leaning on me warming my delicacy of emotions arousing my empty heart

I can't do this

I have to remain touchless

His devilish kind words, his openness to me, to my want, and my needs astonishes me

It makes me want more; more almost unending, never ending, like forever scared

Scared of what I've always wanted has come about

Scared because this is too good to be true

I settled for a way of life that I popped Prozac and Zoloft and I settled for a routine unemotional lifestyle

That my dogs feel my longing to be touched they sit with me and cuddle

Isn't it sad that they are my crutch?

Yet, now there is someone who does these things out of the kindness of his heart

His way for filling my heart: it fills me with warmth and certainty

But it hurts here; it hurts because my mind plays me with the thought of being indefinite

Could I trade everything to just get this?

Is he only doing this as he see fits?

A man of incredolous power

May we remain friends, phamily, and leave the rest in the ditch

He's still a man

He still has Ventures to complete

No one wants to be a pawn: definitely not me

This could be flawless, yet, I failsafe I don't know how to rectify this case

To resist is too late to have been touchless

Little did I Know

Little did I know I feel strongly for you

I'm indulged in your love

I am in pain to love you

Why is this so hard?

Why is my attitude so unstable with you

I can't help that I don't like anyone you know, but you're so social

I used to be that way and I'm trying so hard to go back to it

Little did I know that I will cry to want you back so bad

Away you have gone

A step out is where you are and I am NOT to follow

I feel I'm going in a windmill with air around me becoming tighter and unneeded to live without you is creating bruises on my body

Little did I know

I still think I cannot meet your standards

Not mine either and no one in my heart

But I'm trying to not let my emotions tear us apart

I'm so sensitive

Devastated.

Curiosity

If you are who I think you are

Then it wouldn't be such a question

This mask that you hide with is so unnecessary

I would love to see what's hidden inside your qualities

I would be the step to pride for you

If I could touch you

You were beside me then you were gone

You made my night and then you vanished

I seen you move your body so gentle

So vibrant and so smooth

You surrounded yourself with me then you moved to another world.

Rough

I struggle to stay afloat with this irritating relationship.

You're annoying yelling, your ungratefulness, and your comparisons.

This anguish of us going back and forth; this outplacement of rolls between who does what.

Why do you even compare our status to your friends?

Why do you show me as a trophy in public then dust me off as a bunny in private?

Are your video games more important?

Are your friends the center of attention in your mind?

I believe our priorities to one another are off.

I believe this rough patch needs to be fixed.

There is no reason for us to be going through so much turmoil when we are supposed to be as one.

You were my dream come true; The Love of my Life.

I shouldn't be saying "were", I should be saying "are".

But dreams happen even when imagination is at its worst, but nightmares control the mind.

Dreams give hope or give fear and in the anguish I'm in, I'm scared.

I admit from my heart: I love you so much.

Yet this combination of us is so rough.

The Blood in My Hand

No one can judge you by the way you feel

If you have a break down or emotional distress Let it ride

Find a place to relinquish the sorrow

No one can critique your writing

It's your emotions and your peace of mind to be released on paper

With the fire in my heart

I hold this piece of glass in my hand

And grasp it for relief of pain

This is my tears

This is reason the blood is on my hand

Feeling the pulse in my hand match the one in my heart

Feels entirely too good

I can't pretend to be something I'm not

But I can build myself to something to be

As long as I don't let go of my expectations of life,
my hopes and dreams all will be well

Keep my hand intacked with this glass

I squeeze a little tighter Yea

I am having one of those moments not of hate

But of the times

I need to be myself: just me and music

As you watch the blood Fall

My sick ways increase as so my depression

I ache of no satisfaction of love

It's been to long

My drink something strong

Something hypnotizing

I need a drink cause your criticizing is erking me

Yet, enough off the side

I sip my blood from the taste of irritation

You might not believe me but I'm so serious

Doesn't matter if you don't notice m

I'll still bleed

I have caressed and stolen grief

For this tear coming from my eye

I grab the aid kit and wrapped my agony with a band aid

I cultivate and mold the blood in my hand

Misaddition

If I told you I didn't know how I felt right now, would you believe me?

I think sometimes everything is so right, but then I trip myself and it in my mind

It all goes

I have a habit of second guessing myself.

Why am I here?

Why is it that I jeopardize my happiness?

It's has nothing to do with love or being with someone

It's what's in me

I can't conquer the internal lack of conspiracy with trust for others in my heart

My own thoughts offend me

I terrorize my heart

The painting I have of how my whole life is supposed to be and how it is supposed to play out: is, but isn't coming together

It could if I could get rid of this uneasy doubt I have

I just don't want to be like everyone else

I want everything to work

I want everything to be solid: loyalty to all extent

I fall back on some things, but my heart is aching with doubt

It is not supposed to hurt and feel this way but it does

The clouds are a crashing skull for restoration on how to love and compromise

I've accepted what love is building to, but forever is a long way and with each other we must keep climbing to fall deeper in love

You secure me through all obstacles

I put my heart out for you

Will you hold it gently and give me TLC for all time

Can you sustain our togetherness for eternity?

Without you I feel untied

I need you to complete me

Red tear drops

Being insecure causes of rumble of regret love and animosity

To think your man is cheating cultivate a hardcore inquiry of the mind

The heart races when his phone goes off every time

The tears fall when you leave him and have time to yourself to think what could he be doing in his free time

One girl that he works with he watches while you talk and she stares at both of you well you talk is creepy

Later you contemplate these actions over and over which you know he's unaware of you seek counsel from a veteran soul and all they say is let it go

Regardless of their antics you cry

You cry because you hurt from this unqualified insecure thoughts that pound into your head

You cry so abrupt that the tears in Redding your eyes

You cry with your soul shaking because you don't know what to believe or do

I cry red teardrops because my insecurity has taken over my accusations our wrong but it still hurts because now I know that you would never mess with no bop

That you love me and I'm in love with you for the sake of me crying with red teardrops

Away

You're not that far from me

Yet you're somewhere else

I want to see you so badly, but I don't want to in
barge in the place that you're located

I want to touch your face and keep my hands
around your shoulders and be close to you

I want to put my nose to yours and never stray from you

If I'm outside you're inside and there's this
clashing feeling that I miss you so much

Yeah, I know sometimes it's your way, but I feel to be close to
you a couple of feet to 50 yards I still feel away from you

Subconscious

I keep having these nightmares: these nightmares of you breaking my heart

I wake up at 3:57 a.m. cuz I'm scared to go back to sleep

I feel like I want to cry cuz in real life, unlike some people, it's my worst fear

I dream of me being jealous with you complimenting and giving more attention to other females while I'm with you

Every once in a while I dream of hating you in the midst of you ignoring me: me running away and come back to see you've left me

I come back and not more than hours later and you've moved on

My reaction is making me shake and I: with almost no hesitation: wake from my sleep

Like I said its 3:57 a.m.; As soon as I looked at the time my head hurts

But I woke myself so I couldn't continue this nightmare

I didn't want to know what would happen next time in the dream if I climbed the stairs to see you and her

I had to wake myself cuz in my dream I carried a .380 Smith and Wesson and knowing my Italian ways in a dream and in real life

I woke myself cuz I know subconsciously I would have blew both ya'lls chest in fanatically

Be safe : don't react

The last part was not in the dream it was the next part to most likely take place

Only the part about us being torn apart because you lost your love for me and abandoned me right in front of other people with no hesitation

I feel I need to ease my pain itself: I feel so hurt that I had this nightmare

I'm lost and I want to cry so badly, but the hate in me as I wrote, grew less

I don't know why you're leaving me and breaking my heart is in my subconsciousness

What are you Protecting

By all means smile in my face; lie cause I'll greet you and keep on walking

If you do know something, the truth and hide it from me I can feel it

You show that somehow you feel sorry for me

But you let every day pass and hide some info that emotionally affect me or ravish my heart to pieces don't lie to me

Tell me we're amazing and everything is going to be ok

It will last forever but inside you

You know I'm giving my heart for nothing

How do you let game be ran on a friend?

If you tell me the truth

Quit pretending we can both go our separate ways

I'll never trust you again

And all ties will be crushed : Tarnished

Deleted just like you and the rest from my life

Please don't be afraid of the consequences that will take place

It's only for the greater good

Your conscience maybe untruced

And reflection, but your honest word has ended all friendship between your friend, you, and me

Who are you protecting?

Save myself

Where is my mind at this point in time

Am I drained

Am I lost somewhere that annoyance veil – me – not me trying to be –

Be nice be calm

But hasty my mind rolls like writing a psalm

What for

What is

Ugh

Me: I have an accordance of dislike

I feel hatred toward myself

Some indefinite sorrow

I can't place the thought nor frustration

But it is there

I fell like I'm trying so hard to live to my standards that I'm failing some way

I need to find my hidden grudge

To release it and move forward

Saving my emotions from turmoil and distress!

Save myself!

Yes I hung up on you

You text me cause you seemed kind of mad?

O – I hung up on you – yea –yea you had an attitude it seemed
while you were talking about absolutely nothing

You were angry and I was frustrated

I guess that comes with not seeing you for a whole day

I was uneasy cause you owe me an explanation
of why you haven't shown me any TLC

No, no, don't call me back: texting will do because I'll just press ignore.

Yea, another way to hang up on you.

No, it's not that your voice is aggravating, it's just makes me
irrational to know that you can call and sound non shalant
like I haven't been thinking about you this entire time.

Wait

Stop calling me and keep texting cause if we speak we might start
arguing and I can't stand when you raise your voice at me!

Really; you can help to when you "think" I'm acting ignorant.

Well that's too bad cause the next thing I can do
until you get here is turn my phone off.

POWER DOWN!

Beware Of Notification

I Am The Witness Of News

I Will Tell You The Truth

Everything You Need To Know

All The Thoughts That Your Mind Need To Rotate The Ups The Downs And What Is Happening

Words To Be Done

A Blatant Task For Awareness

Keep Your Eyes Open To A World Expanded Place

Your Option For What Needs To Be Said

Time Is An Awareness

As You Scribble Your Pen

Tik Tok

Word For Word

Details Of Your Job Give In To The Checklist

You Must Achieve

Look At Me As Your Pen Goes In Rotation

Beware Of Notification

From me to you

Dear sweet heart

My love for you is strong

I've convinced myself I was in love with you

But I didn't get nothing out of it now

You've moved forward and I'm left behind

I'm breaking down

And is lost as ever

For the truth to be told

I don't know what to choose

I don't know how to feel

You were my light and my love

It kills me inside to know you really never cared

I'm sorry for myself to be here

I could say love was blind

Even though love was never there

Your fatal attraction to me I don't know you

Past tense is all i can express

Our relationship is gone in the wind

I hope you take part of my letter from me to you

I'm expressing these words for you to understand

That all it turned out to be broken dreams and a tunnel of dirt

Tell me how do you cheat on someone you claimed you love

Proves you were fake and I wasn't good enough

I'm a gangsta and swore to my self

I'm too good to cry but when it comes down to it

I cried like an infant getting an IP shot

Instant pain is what it turned out to be

I have myself set to cruise

Take my time and slow down

I know you looking at this and it's killing your heart

But then again, you never cared, so forget you

Forget what we were

I can't it's here in my heart

A broken hear from you

Your nerve really experienced pain in this relationship

But me

I did

Trust me

I'll never forget

When you look at me after you read this

See the hurt

Look deep

From me to you

I hope you feel my hurt one day cause the pain won't go away

Find yourself out and take notice to what you've done to me

In the future recognize the signs

Read in between a players lines

I still feel used

And it's from me to you

I'm sorry I was late

So many things had to be done today

I'm tired

My feet hurt and I know I need to get dinner done

I done know I have to take care of you

I'm sorry I'm late

Everything is not always my fault

I'm doing all I can to make sure we are secure for life

I can't make mistakes just because I'm rushing

If I rush I won't get nothing done correctly

I am trying my best to be on time at all times

You my love are my number one priority

And from my heart I give you whatever you need to have access as long as I uphold my time to you

I will be sure to be by your side on the dot of time

Even though space and latitude keeps us apart

In my mind

You are constantly rotating in the mist of any occasion

For us to be aligned together as one in fate

I'm sorry my sweet love

I was late

The one that got away

To be friends with someone you may have ended
up with as a love is a very rewarding feeling

To know that they are ok with the choice you made was not
them is simply a best friend with no strings with a nice end

The part of them knowing you better than
the choice you made is rather sad

The one you chose doesn't give the same effort or care
things you have to say unlike the one that got away

Confused that your bestie can pin point every
emotion you are feeling and always in the end of the
conversation makes you feel a bit of regret, but has
all the mood swingers to make you feel better

They're encouraging to your life and heart and yet you
can't have them because you've made your choice

Inside, no matter what; the one you chose, you love, and pray
that your relationship can somehow eventually be the same way

To hurt inside for truth that you will never have
a friend like the one that go away

Your number one friend, who you know can handle anything in your
life you tell, your nasty, spoiled, crazy attitude

Make it like it was

Have we came this far to be so silent?

Do we repeat stuff over and over like we've been together for ages?

I really hope this isn't a dry patch for us.

Can we not speak because we have no real events going on?

I feel so bad because we have no words for each
other, but words for everyone else.

Is this so difficult that we can only send three
word messages to one another –

We can't have fallen off

We can't break up just because we're far away from
one another and our lives are repetitive

Why can't it be like it was where we talked about random stuff?

The conversations where we were endless with our notions of life.

I hope our infatuation hasn't left.

Sleepless nights thinking about you hugging my
pillow wishing you were with me - is it me?

Am I making you miss the old us?

Cause I miss it.

I hate being irritated talking to you.

Let's start over or press the restart button cause I hate to fuss.

I just want to make it like it was.

Soul redemption

Past romances I dare not say: I sacrifice the memories for you.

Flings abroad in my life I shall not compare to you.

The things I've did to former crushes~I will never repeat to you.

You are what captivates my inner being.

For even the smallest unexpressed emotion that I choose to hide.

To assure you of all Love that I give you.

This is my soul redemption.

On the zone of where my potion of cravings for you it is my unmistakable pension.

I could not compare you... Again I say...

You have this everlasting touch to my skin that melts my world into blubber.

The smallest smile you show me will be forever grinning in my eyes.

For my un-honest trusts and half-witted answer.

I portrayed my emotions in our talks with your grace in your decision.

You are my man.

I release the honest self-redemption.

To be angry with you for no reason at times.

To be a bum and show no smile or interest towards when I am upset is my down fall and my uneasy sorrow.

I'd cut out my heart with correct & great precaution.

To ask to share our love for one another with my soul redemption

Love is just a word

IT'S A PLACE OF TORMENT CONFUSION

WHY IS IT SAID

HOW DOES IT MAKE YOU SECOND GUESS LOYALTY

WHY DOES IT SEEM TO LEAD TO HEARTACHE

ITS UNATTRACTIVE AND UNREAL

WHEN SAID; IT'S SO FAKE

AND WHO SAID IT IS FULL OF IT

AM I TO STAND THE LIE YOU CREATED

IS YOUR STEP TO FANTASY ANY BETTER THAN LOVED

USED TO CREATE ANIMOSITY

USED FOR YOUR FEELING

I'M LOST ABOUT THAT WORD

I DESPISE THE TONE ITS EXPRESSED

YOU ARE WHAT YOU SAY

BUT THE ACTIONS ARE NOT THERE YET

LESS TO HOW YOU RENEGE

LOVE I'D UNCONDITIONAL

LOVE ISN'T FATE

BUT LOVE ALWAYS TURNS TO HATE

JUST AS FAST AS THE FEELINGS COME AS SWIFT AS A HEART BEAT THEY CAN GO

What about me

What about me is it that you dislike?

I try my best with effort into do what society says I'm supposed to do, but it's tiresome as if I'm not getting any help

This isn't the fifties anymore and I'm not a maid

That was for women with no job and stay home

So what about me?

Am I not good enough that you have to turn your head or comment on other women better than me?

Do my parents disgust you to where you prefer to be away from me as if there's no chance in your heart to be happy with one person?

Many, many people lie everyday is a day they love someone or do you just love me because of the basic things I do and dismiss everything else

what about me do you not understand is shy and antisocial around people who I have nothing in common with?

I learned long ago there's no reason to talk if there's nothing in common and it's starting to hurt because that's where we seem to b?

So explain to me what it is about me that you married in love cuz the way this is going isn't going right

Maybe we should agree to disagree since you can't say what you don't like about me

Breathless

No one is more destructive than me

They say that people have failures happen to them
due to another's greed for self-loathing.

To rebuild from forced pain an undeniable acquired hate.

What is there to live for when the one who you
thought loved you throws you in the shadows.

His wants cast you into the darkness of the selfishness of the
ocean who captivates everything and drowns it or let's it swim.

He force you to drown took everything and even
your head smashing it in the current.

You couldn't come up to circulate air in your
lungs, in pain, lifeless, with no air.

He drowned too much giving and still you
were suffocated to be with someone.

I'm grateful to be happy and learn of the lie.

The lie you've been used for.

He used you.

You're supposed to laugh and be in love.

You're supposed to give everything, but when giving is empty to
the other who is sucking life out of your heart... You just can't.

He may have thought he left you live with, but in all:
you are rebuilding from being breathless.

Roll up the window

So you trying to hold a conversation while I'm mad?

You trying to explain yourself while I'm pissed off about your playercard?

You think I'll just sit here in my car and wallow in sadness about your hoes?

You got me twisted and there's no way you can talk to me because you suck!

Your voice is annoying.

You lie coninuously and I can't support that.

So I feel the need to roll my window up.

Why you mad?

Why you shouting out words like I did you wrong?

I did my part as the wife.

I gave my heart and served you, but you didn't become the ideal man because you were to the point where you were at your best... with your friends

You did yourself a favor and pushed me away and didn't give a single concern which is leaving us in a rut.

So I'm doing you a favor and slowly driving off and rolling my window up.

Never have to be alone

After marriage takes place you take a grasp of having someone by your side.

You have a partner to assist, encourage, and give you their time of day:

Yet deep into it you notice that it isn't what tale tells from child stories on TV

It's not Disney

It's not Cinderella or Snow White

Being married is what you make it and right now with your career consuming, it turns out to be boring.

It's sad when one spouse is trying to do what is supposed to be done and the other still live somewhere in the past

The goal of this union with to never be alone

You talk to your best guy friend more than you talk to me everyday on the phone

Who am I?

I am the invisible, the maid that does everything practical in the house;

I am not a woman who lives at home with no job.

I'm not a jobless wife with no future, but to serve her husband

To have almost nothing in common is a slight sadness that can't be overcome if there's no effort.

Separate TVs, seperate offices in our house does not defeat the thoughts of never having to be alone

Intimacy

I HAVE HAD SO MANY THOUGHTS ON MY MIND FROM THIS STRIFE THAT I COMPLAIN TO MY HUSBAND ABOUT.

MANY WOMEN DO FEEL THE SAME

NO DOUBT ABOUT IT

TO HAVE A NON-EMOTIONAL MIND IS ABSURD

IT DOESN'T MAKE ANY SENSE

THE THOUGHT FOR HIM TO GO TO COUNSELING TO GET SOME GUIDANCE ON HOW A WOMAN SHOULD BE TREATED IS WORTHLESS

HE THINKS HIS ATTITUDE IS JUSTIFIED BECAUSE HE IS A MAN

WHICH IS NOTHING OF THE LIKE?

INTIMACY IS NEEDED IN ALL ASPECTS OF A RELATIONSHIP AND I DON'T GET WHERE HE SITS WITH THIS NO TOUCH PRODIGY

HE SITS AND CALLS ME A BABY

SAYS I ACT LIKE A CHILD BECAUSE I LIKE TO BE TOUCHED

BECAUSE I LIKE TO BE HELD

BECAUSE I LIKE TO BE THE CENTER OF AN ATTENTION BY THE MAN I LOVE

LOVE IS NEVER ENDING CORRECT

AND IN ORDER TO KEEP IT THAT WAY

TO KEEP A WOMAN ALIVE IN A RELATIONSHIP IS TO BRUSH HER WITH WHAT SHE NEEDS... INTIMACY

A FEELING SHE IS LOVED, IN PUBLIC IN PRIVATE IN THE SMALLEST WAYS

TOUCHING PRECEDES THIS ACCUSATION OF HOW LOVE SHOULD BE

YES MEDIA AND VISUALS OF OTHERS... GIVE THIS TO WAY TOWARD THE MINDSET OF ROMANCE

THE MAIN THING THAT LACKS IN A NON-INTIMATE SITUATION

THIS TURMOIL IS VICIOUS

THIS FEELING OF ABANDONMENT IS NOT GOOD FOR A RELATIONSHIP

TO BE CARESSED AND WARM IN THE ARMS OF THE ONE WHO LOVES ME

HE DOES NOT SHOW ME THIS.

HE IS LIKE SUCH A KING WHO HAS RANDOMLY HAD HIS BRIDE CHOSEN BY ANOTHER AND OFFERS TO CARE AND TAKE CARE OF ME BUT TREAT ME AS IF I'M THERE BUT NOT THERE.

IT IS A GIVEN TITLE THAT I AM HIS WIFE, BUT NOT EMOTIONAL.

LOVE CANNOT LAST FOR THE GREATER GOOD OF JUST SAYING WHO I AM AND NOT SHOWING IT IN PUBLIC.

AM I JUST A GIVEN STATUS TO HIM

AM I JUST AN ARM PIECE?

HIS PASSION IS NOT ME

HIS HEART IS NOT ME

I AM ALONE TO PLAY WITH MY DOGS BECAUSE THEY SHOW ME MORE LOVE.

HOW AGGRAVATING IS THIS.

I FEEL LIKE I'M JUST TAKING UP SPACE IN MY OWN HOUSE.

I DO WHAT IS REQUIRED OF ME AT THE MOST WHEN IT COMES TO CHORES.

YET I AM STILL LEFT EMPTY

I REMAIN TO THE LICK OF MY DOGS AND MY PEN AND PAPER

TO SIT ALONE FOR MANY NIGHTS AND PONDER WHAT I AM MISSING

TO FIND OUT WHAT IT HAS TURNED TO BE THIS NULLING VACANCY

I THE WIFE OF A GREAT MAN IS LACKING IN EMOTIONS

SOMETHING THAT NEEDS TO BE FREE

A QUARREL OF DEFICIENCY

I LACK THE WORLD OF INTIMACY

Ignoring love

From the first put down you threw in my face:

I felt below what a wife should feel or how she should be treated.

The way that you speak to me with a sloppy friend dialect:

It seems you take me as a maid and advantage of me as if I'm here to just do as you please for your benefit.

Am I supposed to have a to do list for you that I do?

I don't mind it;

I enjoy being a wife, but your actions and sly ways make me feel unappreciated.

We don't have children, but dogs. You talk to me the same as them.

I'm not a robot, but that's the mode I've fallen into.

Why?

I do not understand.

I was lovable, lively, and social in the beginning.

Yet, now I'm under a bushel of degenerate words and loath from you.

I felt scorned in my soul with the times you've blocked me from the world.

Where do we go for me to admit this other then above?

it just proves you don't want me and have ignored love.

What can never be

To replace what I have would alter this entire world.

To manipulate time and space for someone who appears to care about me.

But me? Like him more than he likes me?

That could end in tragedy.

The words I love you and play siblings couldn't mean more than anything to him.

To use me for his special time only when he is available is a cold realization.

How could he want me and not know too much about this life?

How much I feel that no one in this world shows me more attention than he does.

All he sees is the sad female who is shallow with no happiness and that's me.

It is apparent that I'm not good enough nor is he on my intellectual level to care.

I am torn from what is happening and what could happen

He holds me in his arms with true meaning, but disappears like lightning in the sky

He is the man with the say so.

He shows me what it is to be free, yet he admits with his eyes and his actions what could never be.

Difficult

The thoughts that generate within our minds
concur with what we want as a person.

We sit and talk about, describe, what
we see and what we need, but never
take the time to go after it.

We text, but never call, we hold in
feelings, but never express them.

Why is the possibility to be rejected so hurtful?

Shouldn't it be a form of courage that One
took initiative to step up and say something.

Love is difficult to attain a
crush from a distance.

Love is difficult to gravitate towards
if you're afraid to love and your heart
holds no loyalty with insecurities.

You can't be in love with someone
from a distance and be happy.

You either love them to let them go
or stay in denial with a dream in your
soul that you can never let go.

Your heart will stay soft as you sulk.

But by far you cannot stand in solitude
with yourself if you make love difficult.

Ever after

Should it be the last

Could it be the beginning

Where does it come from

And how does it start

It is anonymous

Yet I feel abrasive to its attraction

This place will make one seem desperate

This place is quite worthless piece of ...

Insane asylum

To what grimy allusion do I owe it

The subject

The truth

The always wanted

But always cause pain

Whoever said

Love was worth agony

Many people

But its unconvincing

The end of the road

For time to continue life is only a grasp of air

It is what people consider a step of light

But where does it all go?

Emotions?

Proof of work:

Achievements – what do we do to get through life and wither: be happy in retirement or die working to provide to meet the standard of lifes cycle.

Full fledged understanding of living

Labor for a family Labor to survive

Aging greatly – wrinkles, stress, complications, remedies

Creating generations providing ethics one to one passing some sensible jargon to keep us on a path.

From babies to adults to elderly

Yes: gray hair, arthritis, cans, wheel chairs.

Retirement in good health ending in wealth for the up coming

To what is greatly appreciated: Some succeed

Some crumble into debt

Good management

Timing for the last breath of taking souls

This is the place

The death bed

Hmmm

The end of the road

Wasted my years

You said I was yours, yet you stop treating me so.

Love is destruction inside of a soul to promise eternity and drop it at a half a split second is insane.

I've giving you my all and you threw it under a train.

You emotionally taped my mouth shut, taped my hands together, and taped my feet together.

Why on earth claim me for so long and throw me to the Wolves alone, uncertain and to die.

In my mind there is so much hatred because you let our love die.

It wasn't my fault.

Do not let this mistake of separation take place.

After that I gave over a hundred percent, but maybe you need more from me or maybe you were taking advantage of my heart.

I thought maybe I could give you everything you needed, but I guess my all didn't seem to be enough.

Maybe me showing pain in my attitude gave more away than the small words I said to you.

By all means if you want nothing to do with me

I wish you would have noticed in the beginning

But you let it ride, and we all know we can't get back our time.

So with this glass full of liquor, in tears I toast you.

Cheers for all my wasted years

People change

To go from solid and fall apart

Where indications may lie

To mature

To rise in a better place

Rebuilding an emotional wreck can indicate some motivation above the rest of broken hearts

There is light that spreads rays from the sun

But only a person who alternates his ways can go forward to it

Distance and time is a hard era to have between lovers

Trust

Trust

Trust

Loyalty and fidelity

An emotional thought can hurt a heart by the thoughts of past pain

Past pain

Can be the worst earthquake in life

Shifting some internal clock from smiling

To a crushing blow of anger and disturbance some way somehow the whole world has emotional disruption but there's always some kind of spirit that can switch modes and affect the skeptical heart in range

Yet for better or worse through time, space, soul, life, building, worlds together, and love increasing.

People change

Fearful

My conscience aches for some type of remedy

My muscle rocks with adrenaline for what is to happen

The incorrect ways of some passion is blatantly untold

Who are you to judge my temperate of love?

Who is the one who will open my hands and give me forever?

I shun to the thought of some imperative notion of my
forever to be complete with the person I need in my life

But fearful I stand to what all odds that is to come
against the sturdy life I have for myself

The Throne I built for my achievements has
me standing in an empty hole

I have unintentionally I dug myself to hide in

I shiver to be found and brought the truth

Sometimes truth does hurt and love does too

I wait for the one who will stand beside me to rule

But as of now I still am lost unimportant and fearful

Ex

I never knew pain until I met him.

I never lied to myself until he lied to me.

A fabricated happiness to brag and to tell all my friends what a great boy friend he was.

I was forever mind settled that it was the place to be and not be alone.

In the end of those times I was hurt - destroyed and confused.

Lying gets no one anywhere but broken and that's what my fragile heart was.

I've learned my lesson.

The ex always leaves an imprint of distress.

That's what it is of course my heart become hard and so did my view towards the thoughts of love.

It was the relevance to never move on to the next.

But my heart is now captivated by a fantastic man, so I am completely free of the thoughts and past violation from my ex

On defense

I wish I spoke like I write

I've learned to answer in need of a question.

I talk less than what's needed of me.

My vocabulary is so full yet my communication level is not.

I would love to talk about many topics from how splendid the ocean I've been to vacation to the cities I've traveled and enjoyed seeing new things

But is my conversation a nuisance?

I'm opening to speak and smile which makes me happy

I don't always seclude myself anymore

I need to be freed from this animosity against life to smile

To smile is to be free.

I can't be happy if I don't let myself be.

One can choose to be happy.

To average myself from pain is to let go of past emotionally injuries.

To smile is possible out take and intake.

I can't hide.

I can't keep being on defense I am to release this awkward hate that surrounds me.

I write to get rid of it but in a way it motivates me...

Yet it's killing me.

Guilty of my nonchalant attitude guilty of being angry with the world but why?

Why did I make myself a target for misery?

I just jumped to defense

I'm changing

I'm open to a new me

I lay down my sorrows and greatness of me I present

I can quit this unnecessary self defense

Hes not coming

I sit in pain to expect your face

I watch the area you usually would come to get me

Are you mad at me

Have you left me out to dry

My soul feels sorrowful because my tears burn from missing you so

I can make accusations and think all types of things

But when it comes to the last minute

No matter what

You'll remain in my heart

I peek up again with hope to hear the sound of your boots, but... just like silence in the desert

I hear nothing

I have to leave soon and I'm so scared to.

I don't want to miss you stopping by and I hurt at the thought of not seeing you

I guess I've waited too long and the sun has tanned me some

This poem is rather emotionally numbing in my mind

All I can say is hes not coming

Let me go

I feel the world is off balance

I think that people are so confused to the lacerations of life

It is in my perception that people are just so slow; they know absolutely nothing

And refuse to listen to the truth

How ignorant can you get

People say the dumbest comments and complain about the problem

When in all research and considerations

They can fix it themselves, but NO!

Everyone wants it their way

They want to be taken care of.

In this place of hate, torment, criticizing, lying, and constant two faced friendships...

Love does not exist

People wonder why attitudes and rejection is spread and given so easily, but in their own lifestyles they might have all in steady

But all is pronounced in broken hearts, broken promises, misusing, lies... and this is why love isn't nothing

Why are we dying –emotionally – that forth worthless word Love – If I hate that word then why would I be friends with you?

Why would I show and open my heart?

Why would I waste my time?

The way everyone acts is selfish and eventually easily forgotten?

Not in this world

Love has no say

Compassion has no helping hand

Begging and broken dreams are political: brought hands out.

Instead of going out to get the educated heads up in any purpose or situation;

Keep tearing down;

Keep running your mouth keep supposing you might do something.

Shut up and take the chance

Do what you can do, if it don't work kick rocks and try something new.

Knock on wood!

And you might turn some successes.

Quit complaining! Cause all you're doing is biting the hand that feeds you.

Then expect one day,

To be cut back cut off and be let on your own loss:

Hey, this is only my thoughts... that's why my facial expressions express what seems what the world feels and shows from the shell whole self centered vanquished home.

Please let me go.

Not alone

Not alone

Cry – my eyes water like a raging ocean

I give in to harassing thoughts of ending of my happiness being drained

The taunts of unplenished love

Someone – someone like me can't hold my breath forever

To wish for serenity in this world

No compassion

No trustworthiness

Who did wrong

Iniquity

Brought to a peaceful world

Turmoil in my soil granges upon a bath of hate

This outlook as I stand by myself

I cannot be the only one

I cannot have these specific thoughts for abandonment for love

Our childhood

Were we sold many dreams depression of our trust is remarkable

People say we're diterating

But who judges?

Everyone

Is America the court of blamed crimes

Are we raunchy?

Are we indecisive of what happiness really is?

But yet greed has taken us

But yet I'm not alone in my thinking process

Ignore the needy and do you

Get what you need and keep movin

Yet when one feels alone

When one is unhappy

There is bound to be more

No you are not alone

Many can come together and create a complaint with a chorus with grief

Against the system with a captivating song

Wondering eyes

It bothers me that your eyes watch the wrong thing

Yet it's only me

I think you pay attention to what you see in detail to my opinion.

Other females and their swish, other females and their looks;

And other females with their shape.

Jealous I am of these things

I think you look out

Unhappy with what ive come up with

Yet I know you pay attention to everything

All things

Watching your 6 to every degree

But as a man, as you are you are you have known tendencies of wondering eyes

An uncomfortable feeling you give as your eyes drift and your eyes shit in wonderment towards outsiders

My heart of feelings are offended but I cannot control your, eyes

But then again I cannot control my jealousy

Please let this act of disrespect subside

Due

My man –

You

My man

Control your wondering eyes

I shall try to love

To love someone is a beast of an option

Its hard if you don't trust anyone

Im working on it

I may be in this relationship

I may be lovey dovey, but if I question you
then I admit I don't really love you

I don't know what love is

As far as I know you just settled

It hurts myself to think you just settled

I feel like I'm the one with the emotions, but I'm so
emotionally unstable that I see myself with hand nubs

Just helpless.

Therefore I shall I try to love.

Push away

It's amazing how someone doesn't know they're pushing you away, you ask for the smallest things above all else

The repentance request for attention and conversation, some indication that they always are available to care

Never asked for money or materialistic things

Just tender words, words of endearment, words of love, of expression, petting the heart with some type of warmness that assures one it will never grow cold

Or to share this is a heartfelt endeavor

But you notice it is a light warm of attention

Not the one you need or require

Relationships are a compromise: but sometimes it needed to have something out weigh in a particular situation

If a person is feeling lonely, distressed, and out of place

They require some affection

To be rejected of such desire makes feelings decrease into a fade

The worst feeling is to assume ones self pushed away

The moment that is cracked

The heart that shatters from being ignored causes triumph in the hypocrite of love

Who hates to be alone

EVERYONE

All people need some type of reassurance that they are cared for

We are only human, but some people need it more than others

The farther away words and whispers come the more pushed away is a person by a purge of foul stink

The pain it is to let someone go is indeed a crisis, what to do after being shunned in a way you can't stay

You know you shouldn't wait

You might as well say you were pushed away

A.L.O.N.E.

I seem to fight the urge to want to move on

No one has the audacity to throw themselves back into a world wind of estimated questionable pain.

Apart from society that promotes divorce, extortion, exposure and crime.

I prefer to sit in an empty box with a good book and classical music playing in my headphone.

No one wants to put themselves out in the open to a new person who is contaminated by the world too.

Less time to enjoy life and point towards the things that got pushed back due to the unsupportive distraction that took over an empty heart; For that I hate you.

Oppressed by your unemotional word towards my feelings. The flawless carelessness of you saying, "do it on my own", showed that it is a relationship by myself.

Nothing ever was good enough for you, my clothes, my hair, my speech, my friends, so in all... ME! Thank you for nothing.

Empty is what we were from the beginning. Lust is all you saw for me, unlimited sex, because all you wanted was my booty? Right? Just selfish and incentive. So have you learned your lesson now? I'm not alone or lonely. But Hell... I'll leave you alone. Why? Cause I'm gone!

Vacation

I'm tired of sitting around the house all day

I'm overwhelmed by this inaccurate routine that we live

I work out of the home

I work in the home

It's too new to me to even continue this right now

I need to distance myself and get away

Maybe I need the 2 hour relief and go run

To accept this life requires me to get a vacation

My head throbs from day to day events

I feel sick because I can look around my house and see that I am doing everything and over exerting my stress level making it hard to keep up with my happiness.

I dislike having

I'm losing my mind conversations either help me out or let's go on some type of vacation

I may be young, but I have so much responsibility and you act like this a breeze.

Dismissed

You can beg and say you're sorry you can lie and say you didn't meant to

Yes you can lie and say you love me

You can cry and pray you can come back

But realize you can't even accept your own faults, my hate for you is ecstatic

I wish you dead for the pain you caused me

I wish your body mutilated for my embarrassment you threw on me

How dare you treat me like I'm a mistress when my title is your wife?

How dare you call me names for the wretched shit you did you sorry man you're dismissed

I can know longer give you me

You lost me and this marriage with your indisgressions

I can never imagine myself to trust someone else in the anguish you left me in

Strait off pissed

You broke, fake, heartless, boy

You should know you're dismissed

The promises of a man to love me, take care of me and protect me has been flushed in the server

You dared to abandon me the moment I left

Was I a distraction to you in your freedom?

There was no reason to lie and marry me

you did it for show

You ended it embarrassment for both of us

There's multiple issues that we may have had but the loyalty amongst what needed to be done, and your hypocrisy to do as a man, left us in a ditch more me than you

You had your fun while I was in misery

When we finally are completely done

Trust me you will never be missed: I hate you: you are dismissed

Temporary Forevers

Rushing into a life that you want may not be good for the other person

The issues of uncontained selfishness that one may never express because they hide their wants very well

Being happy is the best attribute to hold on too.

You never know a person until you're not around

The time before the eternal distance is something to savor

The screw up in a relationship on a fault of the person who took advantage of the heart and trust has been grounded as a break up

A temporary forever

In the beginning it started as a promise, a swear, a connection of the heart for both people to become one

The spread of the betrayal and soft unmeaning repeat has no remorse in the heart

Take your see saw ways and part

I am too great to be ram sacked and destroyed by you again

You had me at hello and you lured me in very clever

You took my time my love and my money

I disrespected you almost rarely and kept you close and in my prayers

Yet you don't take blame or responsibility for your wrong

In my last words I shall put on my steppers

Your actions and decisions broke us and turned us into a Temporary Forever

All the while

Every time you call I jump to phone, but now I know I'm the princess and I have to leave you alone

In it all you smiled and attempted to care

Yet all the while you were taking my heart, but rejected to share

Lies are the main verbs that come from your mouth

But it seems that's how they do where you're from deep in the south

Dude; you ain't no man

yeah

You got a job but honey you may stay clean but ya game is on slob

Yet somehow I stayed with ya

How idiot of me all this while

Now I can say

"Say bro you been acting like a child"

Me take care of you

Baby let me tell you

That's for a mother to do

I'm your gal I'm your wife

But keep asking for stuff

And its going to be end of this life

Flip the script

No more of our relationship

Shady heart

The shady heart is covered with anguish

The feeling to burst the moment of sorrow

The open hand that was ready for someone special

I found that compassion was in the beginning

The grasp of life revolved and timed itself around you were he in my world

The tension that stood the questions that stayed still

The hate for love and your smile of deception

Where are you

Why did you leave?

Do you not want me as I want you?

My heart is crushed while you have the free ride

Of my fake infatuation

How unsure can love break the cycle of bleeding hearts?

No one can be here with me anymore

There is no trust or taking less than what I deserve

You would not speak of the past

Your unopened kindness can snow the lies of your scars

Thank you for the new world of my extreme
hate because of your shady heart

Chew on this

My husband is jealous of nothing.

He treats me as if I'm around for specific jobs, but being
distant his leash on me causes him to go insane

He acts crazy to no extent and acts like a punk
who can't control their own dog

I was merely a joke to him with the chores I did

I cleaned cooked paid bills and took care of the dogs

I was stuck in the house and there was no where he wanted me go

If I did go out, come back, walk in, he'd be sitting on the couch
watching TV with a drink asking me what took me so long
and ask me did I have fun with my friends more than him?

I have lost myself.

My fun in this marriage is drained like a body loses piss

Chew on this

Musical Genius

You are the light to the music world.

You make music the lively hood of people's soul.

Every beat that passes through the pulse of
your blood is birthed and produced into

Greatness.

Your time and continuous work brings out the unknown.

You are one of a kind with every beat you create:

It is like snowflakes~ all the ones you make can't be the same

Such as you thinking on them away from your keyboard

To recreate; that one is dissolved; and created into a new one

It is an altering ego for this musical data...

As you are~ and ~ your musical symphony

Pressing play through beats=it's hypnotizing

The new song captivates the mind and
brings words and fantasy to be said

The beats are consistent and graceful

One moment it's quiet and the next it's a river of
constant rhythm to put one in place of

tranquility

No matter the genre;

Your beats are peaceful and sound so assertive

You create from your heart where musical essence lies

To procreate!

It just amaze me

You are repetitive for your love of music~

To go and produce for greater heights;

To keep on the beat and never stop~

It is none other than Passion

Obsession to generate melody makes you
superior above the people you know

To raise you beyond every harmony made~

Your music lifts you to the sky beyond the
ozone's into a world of self determination

The sexy master mind of endeavor stepping
into an industry for money and profit

You make the little Producer so astounding and admired

Investing your vivacity, spirit, and intellect:

I know success will come to you in bundles as
you sale your beats and perform in

arenas~

Just because you are the Musical Genius.

Dark Cave

Forsaken the everlasting love shared among us.

You brighten my spirits with a radiant truth that no one
will share aloud. Who are you, but a silent voice which
soothes me and rounds your spirit to my soul?

I am nothing, but an imaginary doll without the prying
you've done to open me within the light.

You've forced me to designate the greatest part is my being
toward a ray of piercing brightness that can't be shut down.

I thank you for being my spiritual eye opener, and I thank
you for shoving me into the darkness where I've learned to
see the glorious bright tunnel at the end of this maze.

I have risen from nothing and roughly climbed out of this cave.